Clinical & Medical Laboratory Scientists

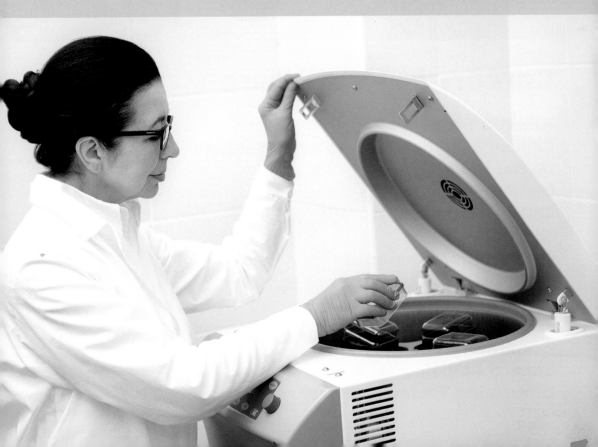

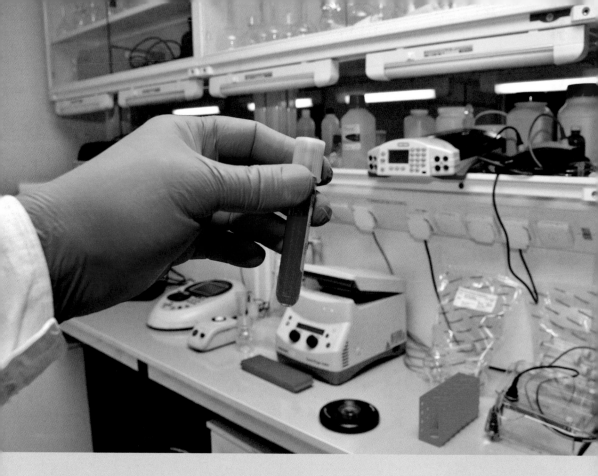

Careers in Healthcare

Athletic Trainers
Clinical & Medical Laboratory Scientists
Dental Hygienists
Dietitian Nutritionists
EMTs & Paramedics
Nurses
Occupational Therapists
Orthotists & Prosthetists
Physical Therapists
Physician Assistants
Respiratory Therapists
Speech Pathologists & Audiologists
Ultrasound Technicians

CAREERS IN
HEALTHCARE

Clinical & Medical Laboratory Scientists

Samantha Simon

MC MASON CREST
PHILADELPHIA

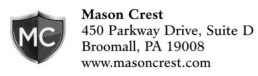

Mason Crest
450 Parkway Drive, Suite D
Broomall, PA 19008
www.masoncrest.com

Printed and bound in the United States of America.

CPSIA Compliance Information: Batch #CHC2017.
For further information, contact Mason Crest at 1-866-MCP-Book.

First printing
1 3 5 7 9 8 6 4 2

Library of Congress Cataloging-in-Publication Data

on file at the Library of Congress
ISBN: 978-1-4222-3796-0 (hc)
ISBN: 978-1-4222-7984-7 (ebook)

Careers in Healthcare series ISBN: 978-1-4222-3794-6

QR CODES AND LINKS TO THIRD-PARTY CONTENT

Table of Contents

KEY ICONS TO LOOK FOR:

Words to understand: These words with their easy-to-understand definitions will increase the reader's understanding of the text while building vocabulary skills.

Sidebars: This boxed material within the main text allows readers to build knowledge, gain insights, explore possibilities, and broaden their perspectives by weaving together additional information to provide realistic and holistic perspectives.

Educational Videos: Readers can view videos by scanning our QR codes, providing them with additional educational content to supplement the text. Examples include news coverage, moments in history, speeches, iconic sports moments and much more!

Text-dependent questions: These questions send the reader back to the text for more careful attention to the evidence presented there.

Research projects: Readers are pointed toward areas of further inquiry connected to each chapter. Suggestions are provided for projects that encourage deeper research and analysis.

Series glossary of key terms: This back-of-the book glossary contains terminology used throughout this series. Words found here increase the reader's ability to read and comprehend higher-level books and articles in this field.

Medical laboratory scientists are often called upon to analyze bodily fluids.

 Words to Understand in This Chapter

biological specimens—living organisms or parts of an organism that are being analyzed or studied.

biotechnology—the study of how life and technology are intertwined.

bodily fluids—fluids that come from a human body.

cell morphology—the branch of biology dealing with cell structure and the classification of cell structure.

medical laboratory technician—an individual who works in a clinical medical lab under the supervision of a medical laboratory scientist.

oncology—the branch of medicine that focuses on cancer and how cancer affects the body.

urinalysis—a diagnostic test, in which urine is tested for various levels of chemicals.

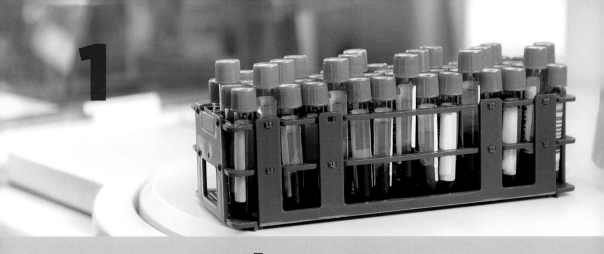

What Do Medical Laboratory Scientists Do?

Whenever a physician orders a laboratory test, whether it is a urinalysis or a blood panel, a medical laboratory technician or scientist is playing a vital role in the step-by-step understanding of those laboratory tests. What medical laboratory scientists provide are answers that help uncover mysteries for physicians and their medical teams about their patients. They do this by performing laboratory tests on human tissue, blood, or other bodily fluids, which give the physicians and their teams a clear picture of the patient's health. These tests offer vital insight into the inner workings of a patient's body and his present health status.

Essential to Diagnosis

Medical laboratory scientists generate key laboratory results that aid in detecting an array of health abnormalities. For example, lab tests can detect diseases such as cancer, heart disease, and diabetes, and could even identify bacteria or viruses in the body. People with these abnormalities could not have been diagnosed without the laboratory testing of their bodily fluids and tissues conducted by a medical laboratory scientist. Once the testing is administered, the results are sent to a physician or someone else on the medical team to use in determining the best treatment. Not only do medical laboratory scientists have to be accurate, they must be able to do their job in a timely manner. A

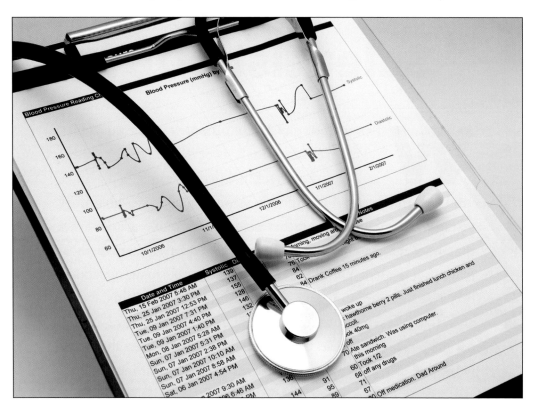

Medical lab scientists collaborate with doctors to help with medical diagnosis.

It is estimated that 70–80 percent of medical decisions made by physicians are a direct result of laboratory test data.

large proportion of diagnostic and medical decisions are based on laboratory test results.

Laboratory testing requires knowledge and education in numerous scientific fields. A medical laboratory scientist has a four-year bachelor's degree in clinical laboratory science. To receive this bachelor's degree, you must take many classes in biology, chemistry, physiology, anatomy, and higher-level clinical sciences. On a normal day, a medical lab scientist will use sciences such as clinical chemistry, hematology, immunology, immunohematology, microbiology, and molecular biology.

"An Experience I'll Never Forget"

A medical laboratory scientist was asked to share a real-life story about an experience she had had with a patient that would stay with you forever. She responded:

"When I started out as a laboratory assistant, we had a young lady diagnosed with AML, acute myelogenous leukemia. I went on two of her bone marrow aspirations. I saw the ups and downs of her condition. I watched as she participated in an experimental drug trial across the state. I called in her critical test results to nurses and empathized with them over her situation. Over a year later, her cancer got worse and she developed various other health issues. One of her last wishes was to marry her high school sweetheart. The staff and nurses of the hospital put on a wedding for her in the garden, just outside the hospital. Pictures and videos of the ceremony were on the news and on our employee website. Tears streamed down everybody's faces as we watched her marry her fiancé. A few days later she succumbed to her illness."

Medical laboratory scientists are also extremely knowledgeable about how to collect and process biological specimens. This means maintaining the chain of collection, keeping the scientist safe, and keeping contamination low. Not only do medical laboratory scientists perform laboratory procedures, they are also required to ensure that the instruments they use are in working order.

These scientists also draw connections between laboratory findings and common diseases or a patient's medical condition(s). Working on behalf of patients, together with the patients' physicians and the rest of their medical teams, they review and interpret test results, integrate data, do problem-solving, and consult on the condition and treatment of patients.

Responsibilities

The primary duties of a medical laboratory scientist include:

- Analyzing bodily fluids, such as blood and urine, and tissue samples; recording normal or abnormal findings; and sending these results to the ordering physicians.
- Studying blood samples for transfusions. They do this by identifying the number of blood cells in a given sample, the cell morphology, or the blood group, blood type, and compatibility with other blood types needed for a transfusion to work properly for the patient.
- Operating laboratory equipment properly, maintaining that equipment, and keeping laboratory equipment up to safety standards.
- Logging the results and findings of laboratory tests and procedures, and discussing them with physicians.

Medical laboratory scientists may conduct research, not

Educational Video

Scan here for information about the medical laboratory scientist career:

only in clinical settings, but in the research and development of new drugs. They may also do research to come up with new laboratory testing and monitoring methods.

The career options for medical lab scientists are vast. Medical lab scientists work in hospital labs and clinics, forensic labs, veterinary clinics, industrial research labs, molecular biotechnology labs, and pharmaceutical labs.

Medical Lab Scientists versus Medical Lab Technicians

A common misconception is that medical laboratory scientists and medical laboratory technicians do the same jobs. This is far from correct. While medical laboratory scientists can perform all tests and procedures physicians order, medical laboratory technicians, on the other hand, cannot perform all these tests and usually work under the direct supervision of a medical laboratory scien-

Did You Know?

According to the U.S. Department of Labor's Bureau of Labor Statistics, medical laboratory scientists earn one of the most competitive salaries among those with a bachelor's-level degree in the nation—median salary: $55,550; national average: $61,860.

There are jobs for labratory scientists in many different types of labs, even in industrial settings.

tist. Oftentimes, medical lab technicians will work for a few years, while still going to school, to gain experience in a lab as they are pursuing their bachelor's degree to become a full medical laboratory scientist.

Medical lab technicians have less schooling in comparison to medical laboratory scientists and also are not as qualified in performing tasks in the lab. Medical laboratory scientists typically must obtain a bachelor's degree in either medical laboratory sciences or clinical laboratory sciences. Medical lab technicians generally need an associate's degree or a post-second-

Did You Know?

Medical laboratory scientists use personal protective equipment, or PPE, including protective masks, gloves, and goggles, to ensure their safety.

ary certificate to begin working in a lab. Some states require medical lab scientists and technicians to be licensed and have certain certifications as well.

Medical laboratory scientists have to be knowledgeable in all aspects of human tissues and human tissue analysis. They might be examining a pediatric sample one day for leukemia and the blood panel of an AIDS patient the next. These scientists are also able to specialize, depending on how large the lab is where they work and their education and training. Some examples of specialties are:

- Immunology technologists, who examine elements of the human immune system and its response to foreign bodies. Hospitals serving many patients with HIV have a tremendous need for these specialists.
- Immunohematology technologists, who collect blood, classify it by type, and prepare blood and its components for transfusions. These scientists usually work for large blood banks.
- Cytotechnologists, who prepare slides of body cells and examine these cells for abnormalities that may signal the beginning of a cancer or a cancerous growth. These scientists often work for large oncology labs or the hospital labs serving oncology wards.

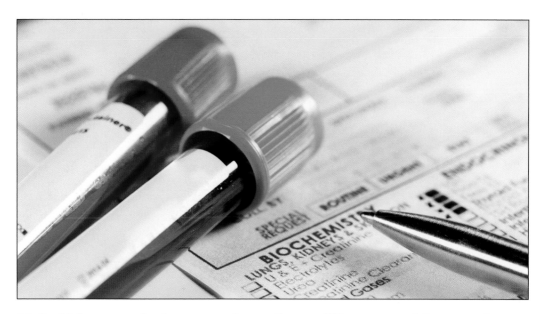

Medical laboratory scientists must understand many different types of diseases and disease states because each specimen is unique and specimens constantly vary.

 Text-Dependent Questions

1. How does the schooling differ for medical laboratory technicians and medical laboratory scientists?
2. What are the various types of bodily fluids and tissues medical laboratory scientists analyze?
3. What bodily fluid do immunohematology technologists work with?

 Research Project

Make a list of diagnostic tests that medical laboratory scientists perform.

Medical laboratory scientists can work in various specialty areas. Some even specialize in the type of specimen they study.

 Words to Understand in This Chapter

autopsy—a postmortem examination of a body and the body's tissues to determine the cause of the death.

blood transfusions—the donation of blood from one human to another; this transfer is monitored medically.

pathogen—a living organism that can cause disease, such as a bacterium or virus.

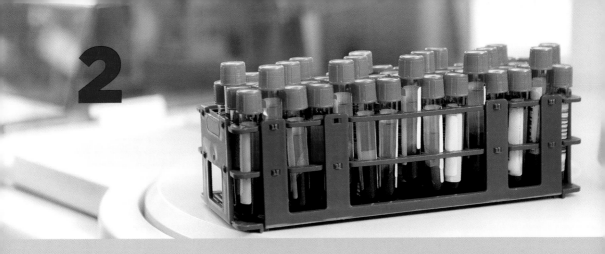

A Look at the Opportunities

Medical lab scientists can choose from among a large variety of specializations and environments to work in. For example, besides hospitals and clinical laboratory settings, medical laboratory scientists can also find jobs in:

- Commercial or reference laboratories
- Public health laboratories
- Pharmaceutical and chemical industries
- Biotechnology companies
- Forensic and law enforcement laboratories
- Veterinary clinics
- Research and teaching institutions

- Transplant and blood donor centers
- Fertility clinics
- Pathology labs
- Sperm banks
- The armed forces
- The cosmetics and food industry

When stepping into the world of clinical and medical lab science, scientists confront various challenges every day. Medical laboratory scientists may deal with three to four different types of bodily fluids and tissue types within a week of work. That is why it is extremely important for these medical laboratory scientists to be extremely knowledgeable about cellular biology and cellular morphology. These scientists are constantly uncovering the mysteries of disease.

Clinical laboratory professionals examine and analyze bodily fluids, tissues, and cells for their chemical constituents. Some specialized scientists also identify blood-clotting abnormalities and cross-match donor blood for transfusions that can be lifesaving. The proper logging of donated blood and blood components plays a major role in any surgical treatment of a patient. In addition to proper logging and testing of blood, these scientists also test patients' blood for drug levels to measure how well particular treatments are working. This lets doctors know if a medical treatment is working at the cellular and molecular level. Medical laboratory scientists evaluate test results and new medical testing processes for accuracy, which then they share with physicians and the whole medical community.

A huge part of the specialty of immunohematology is proper sorting of blood and blood types for transfusions.

Cytotechnologists mainly prepare slides for analyses.

Specializations in the Field

Medical laboratory scientists may choose to specialize in a variety of areas. These specializations open up to medical laboratory scientists an array of different jobs and job opportunities as their career progresses. When you become a medical laboratory scientist, you are taught a vast amount about microbiology and cellular tissue differentiation, so that, throughout your career, you can become even more knowledgeable and decide to specialize in particular areas of practice. You usually pursue specializations after further education, work experience, or certifications. Scientists and technicians may also specialize in one of the many areas of laboratory life sciences. Additionally, medical laboratory technicians can also grow in their career. These technicians can advance to scientist positions after gaining experience and completing additional education and possible certification. Among common examples of specialties within the medical laboratory science field are:

- Immunology technologists, who examine elements of the human immune system and its response to foreign bodies. This specialization is in great demand because understanding of the human immune system is vital for disease prevention and public health. Some of the first disease outbreaks were detected by immunology scientists in clinical labs. These types of medical laboratory scientists generally work for large labs, such as the Centers for Disease Control and Prevention in Atlanta.

- Immunohematology technologists, who collect blood, classify it by type, and prepare blood and its components for transfusions. These scientists usually work for large blood banks. They are called on to properly detect blood type and determine whether or not a patient can receive a *blood transfusion*. They also test blood that is given to blood banks for any blood-borne *pathogens*. And these scientists are integral to the work of most hospitals because they make sure blood transfusions are done correctly.

- Cytotechnologists who prepare slides of body cells and examine these cells for abnormalities that may signal the beginning of cancer or a cancerous growth. These scientists usually work for large oncology labs or hospital labs for their oncology wards. Most cancer can now be detected early at the cellular level. Cytotechnologists are able to detect cancer at these early stages, which can help save a person's life.

- Histotechnicians are scientists who cut and stain tissue specimens for pathologists to read for diagnosis and even *autopsy* reporting. These scientists analyze tissues, both living and dead, to detect different pathologies so they can understand what is going on in a person's body, either during her life or after her life has ended.

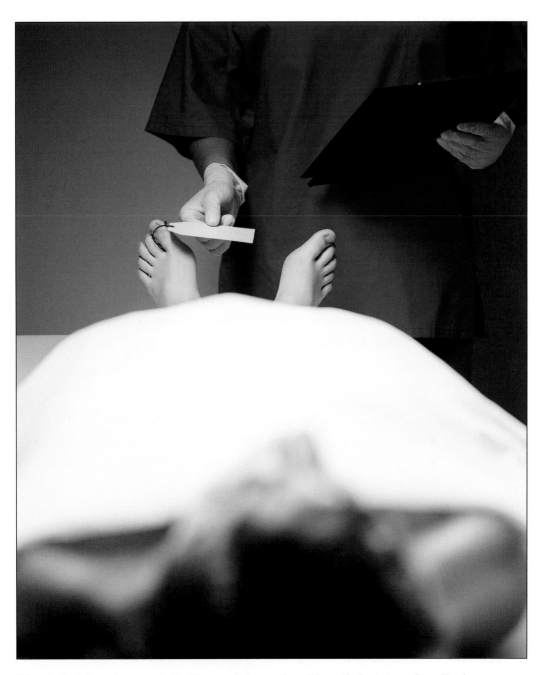

Histotechnicians is a specialty that mainly works with pathologists and medical pathologists in the course of autopsies.

Job outlook

Not only does a career as a medical laboratory scientist or technician offer a large variety of jobs, the number of jobs in the field is continuing to expand as well. With the increase in preventive testing and steady population growth, the need

Educational Video

To see a day in the life of a medical laboratory scientist, scan here:

Did You Know?

Most medical laboratory scientists and technicians work full time, and in various shifts around the clock.

for medical laboratory scientists and technicians is constantly rising. This growth is also due to the development of new lab tests. The Bureau of Labor Statistics projects employment of clinical laboratory technicians and scientists to grow 18 percent between 2014 and 2024. This would create

close to 200,000 more job openings in the United States alone. This is higher than the national average for many careers.

Did You Know?

Medical laboratory scientists and technicians held about 163,400 jobs in 2014, according to the US Bureau of Labor Statistics.

"Friendly and Outgoing"

A medical laboratory scientist working in the field today was asked, "Are there certain specialties within the field that are in greatest demand today and therefore have the most job opportunities and the most job security?" She answered:

> "An MLS who is a generalist is in greatest demand today. Blood bank workers are also in high demand because this is a very stressful job. Off-hour shifts, like overnights, are typically the least desirable and have the most openings. Most jobs offer a pay differential for second and third shifts."

 ## Text-Dependent Questions

1. What is the percentage of projected employment growth in this field from 2014 to 2024?
2. What specialty of medicine do cytotechnologists primarily work with?
3. If a doctor was working with an immune-deficient patient, to what kind of medical laboratory scientist specialist would the patient's lab work be sent?

 ## Research Project

Research additional specialties in the medical laboratory scientist career.

Figuring out the puzzles of diagnosis is a major part of the clinical lab science field.

 Words to Understand in This Chapter

ASCP—acronym for American Society for Clinical Pathologists.

cellular biology—the study of life at the cellular level.

clinical laboratory science—the field of science where medical laboratory scientists work.

practicum—a practical section of a course of study.

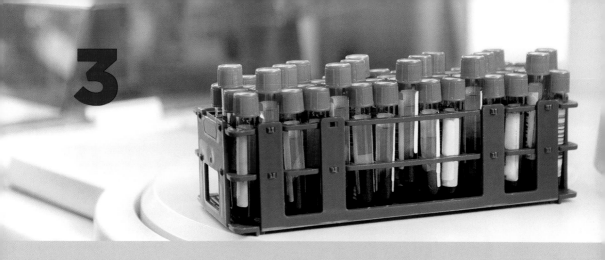

Education and Training

Do you enjoy solving puzzles and problems? Do you like hands-on science? Do you want to pursue advanced studies in science or applied life sciences? Are you looking for variety in your career? If you answered yes to most of these questions, *clinical laboratory science* may be a good choice for you.

When you're thinking about entering the profession of medical laboratory science, the first step is to determine if you would want to become a medical laboratory technician or a medical laboratory scientist. The difference between the two is much more than just education and training. Medical laboratory technicians can work with an associate's degree or a post-secondary certificate, in addition to the correct licensing. Medical laboratory scientists, by contrast, must obtain a bach-

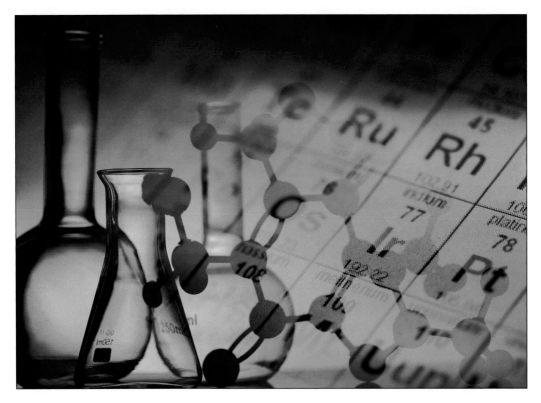

To be certified as a medical laboratory scientist, students must complete their bachelor's degree in an accredited program. Often, they are required to maintain a high grade point average in their science courses.

elor's degree and proper licensing. If you are in high school, and you're interested in pursuing a career in the medical laboratory sciences, you should take classes in chemistry, biology, anatomy, and math.

Medical Laboratory Scientist

Medical laboratory scientists are required to complete a specific medical laboratory bachelor's degree program. These educational programs usually consist of a curriculum rich in chemistry, biology, microbiology, mathematics, *cellular biology*, and other life sciences. In addition to these life science classes, clinical lab and medical lab programs also offer classes emphasizing laboratory technique. This gives medical laboratory scientists a broad grasp of different lab techniques for both animal and human cells, proper

Educational Video

For a short video about the qualities needed for a Med Lab technician, scan here:

use of equipment, and an understanding of lab management and safety procedures. Most programs leading to a medical lab bachelor's degree require students to maintain a minimum grade point average.

Bachelor's degree programs in clinical laboratory science can be offered through a university or by a hospital education program. In university programs, the first year generally puts an emphasis on classes in basic biology and chemistry. During the sophomore year, most universities require students to apply for the medical laboratory science degree program. Once the student is accepted into the program, the following year focuses on upper-level laboratory clinical science courses and *practicum* hours. During this practicum, students work in a series of nearby labs to gain experience and knowledge of laboratory techniques.

Hospital-based programs are usually for students attending a school without an accredited medical laboratory science degree, but have completed the required life science courses, maintained a certain grade point average, and are in the last year of their undergraduate studies.

Medical Laboratory Technician

Medical laboratory technicians have less education and training than medical laboratory scientists; they must be supervised by a medical laboratory scientist. Most receive a two-year associate's degree from a community college in clinical laboratory science or a related field.

During the 1960s, new categories of laboratory workers were created to help cope with the increased workload: the certified laboratory assistant (CLA), with one year of training, and the medical laboratory technician (MLT), with two years of training. Numerous states currently require licensure of laboratory personnel, with others considering it, thus further ensuring the integrity of the profession.

There are a small number of one-year certificate programs for medical laboratory technicians around the country. Most of these programs are offered by hospitals; very rarely, they are available in vocational schools. The admission requirements for these types of programs vary, depending on the program.

Some branches of the armed forces also offer certificate programs for medical laboratory technicians. In these technician programs students are taught practical and generalized lab techniques, especially those applicable to combat situations.

Licensing and Certification

The history of educational requirements for clinical laboratory science has evolved in tandem with the expanding scope of the

Education Overview

Amedical laboratory scientist was asked to describe the education and hands-on training that she received before earning a degree in the field. She replied:

"We are required to have a bachelor's degree. It took me four years, but it may take some students longer. Our prerequisites are similar to those of preprofessional students, like chemistry, biology, organic chemistry, physiology, microbiology, etc. After completion of your prerequisites, you have an interview for the MLS program. You need letters of recommendation as well.

"In the MLS program, you have a rigorous course load. You take classes relating to every part of the laboratory, including clinical chemistry, coagulation, hematology, urinalysis and bodily fluids, microbiology, parasitology, blood banking, immunology, and molecular biology. Laboratory classes are included with each class.

"In your senior year, you have a semester of clinical rotations at a hospital. You rotate from blood bank to hematology, chemistry, and microbiology. Rotations are around eight hours per day and are Monday through Friday. You are graded on technique and knowledge, and you take a practicum at the end of each rotation.

"Before you begin working, you are required to pass a nation-wide licensure test. I took the ASCP, the American Society for Clinical Pathology's exam to be an MLS."

During practicum, medical laboratory scientists have the opportunity to participate in a variety of lab work.

field. In 1930, the American Society of Clinical Pathologists (*ASCP*) issued its first certificates of registration for the medical laboratory field. The requirements for this certification consisted of a high school diploma, completion of one year of classroom work, and six months of experience in a recognized laboratory. As in the field of clinical lab science itself, knowledge started to increase and become more complex. This, in turn, led to more rigorous educational requirements. By 1952, most certifications called for a longer college workload. Most accredited schools required you to have completed three years of college work before you could even begin the certification process. Ten years later, the American Society of Clinical Pathologists' Board of Registry (BOR) made it a national standard to increase the college prerequisite to three years to be able to get a medical laboratory scientist certification.

Today, medical laboratory scientists and technicians can receive a general certification as a medical laboratory scientist or technician. Certifications may also be acquired for subspecialties. Medical lab scientists or technicians must have studied

 Education Differences

Medical Laboratory Scientists

- Four-year degree.
- National degree: clinical laboratory science.
- Educational programs are offered by universities or hospitals.

Medical Laboratory Technicians

- One- to two-year certifications or two-year associate's degree.
- Fewer educational programs.
- Educational programs are usually offered by community colleges.
- Work overseen by a medical laboratory scientist.

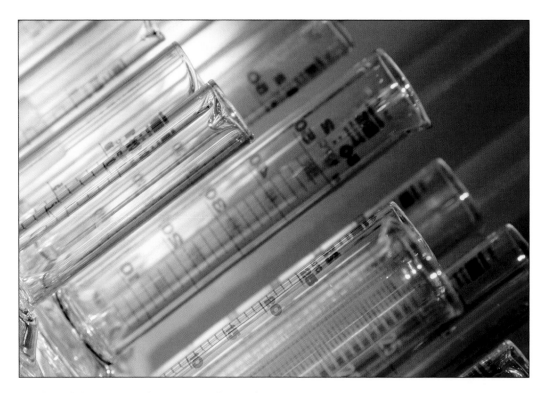

Medical laboratory technicians rank number fourteen in best health care support jobs, according to a recent study by US News & World Report.

or worked for an extended period of time within these specific subspecialties in order to pursue a specialized certification. Specialized certifications may be obtained in a number of subspecialties, including cytotechnology and immunology. To take any accreditation exam, a medical lab scientist or technician must complete a properly accredited medical laboratory program. These programs are accredited by the National Accrediting Agency for Clinical Laboratory Sciences. The American Society of Clinical Pathologists administers certification examinations for both technicians and medical laboratory scientists. Although certification is not required to enter the occupation in all cases, employers typically prefer to hire certified scientists and technicians. In addition to the national certification, 12 states (California, Florida, Georgia, Hawaii, Louisiana, Montana, Nevada, North Dakota, Rhode Island, Tennessee, West Virginia, and New York) and Puerto Rico also require medical lab scientists and technicians to have a state license to practice in a medical laboratory.

Depending on the state, laboratory personnel must be also licensed, in addition to having a certification. Most medical laboratory scientists are licensed by choice. These licensing requirements vary by state, and some states call for licensing if the scientist decides to specialize.

 Text-Dependent Questions

1. Which organization accredits medical lab science programs?
2. In what 12 states do you need a state license in addition to national certification?
3. How many years do medical laboratory scientists go to school for?

 Research Project

Research the nearest medical/clinical lab science bachelor's degree program. What universities in your area offer this program? What is the tuition? What are the requirements to enter the program? What is the curriculum?

The earliest medical labs were usually small corners of doctor's offices.

 Words to Understand in This Chapter

CLA—acronym for certified laboratory assistant.

clinical laboratory—a laboratory where specimens are tested to obtain information about the health of a patient.

diagnostic testing—tests performed to help determine a medical diagnosis.

pathology—the branch of medicine that deals with the laboratory examination of samples of body tissue for diagnostic or forensic purposes, and especially the cause of disease and the effect that disease has on the body and its tissues.

Evolution
of the Profession

Medical professionals have always examined human body fluids, dating back to the earliest days of medical history. The first known clinical laboratory was opened in 1896 at Johns Hopkins University Hospital. This "clinical lab" was a 12-by-12-foot room outfitted with equipment that cost about $50. Before this clinical lab was put in service, most doctors and hospitals used small corners of their offices and hospitals to perform very early lab tests. And most of the time the physicians were performing the diagnostic testing themselves. The thought of having a separate clinical diagnostic laboratory was unheard of in the 19th century and physicians saw this as somewhat of a luxury and out of reach.

Medical laboratory scientists examine different cells and cell forms for pathologists and other doctors.

This all changed as scientists learned more about the causes of diseases. During the nineteenth century, scientists such as the Frenchman Louis Pasteur discovered the connection between microorganisms, which Pasteur called "germs," and sickness. Pasteur carried out a series of simple experiments in the 1860s that showed how bacteria and other organisms were carried on dust particles in the air. He boiled some beef broth, in order to kill any organisms already present, then left it in a glass flask that had a long, narrow neck which allowed in air but trapped dust particles. The broth did not decay. Pasteur's experiments led him to develop his "germ theory of disease," which held that diseases could be passed from one individual to another by the tiny organisms that caused the disease. The germ theory encouraged other biologist to look more closely at bacteria, which were believed to be the carriers of disease. During the 1890s, the first viruses were discovered.

As the medical profession recognized how deadly diseases like tuberculosis, diphtheria, and cholera could spread, doctors put an emphasis on diagnostic testing and the proper handling of bodily fluids to avoid germ contamination. This also prompted the development of tests for the detection of pathogens in the late 1890s.

By the turn of the twentieth century, the laboratory had made its way to the forefront of medicine. At this time, physicians and other medical professionals realized how important a clinical lab really was. This prompted

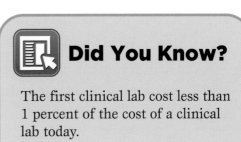

Did You Know?

The first clinical lab cost less than 1 percent of the cost of a clinical lab today.

Educational Video

Scan here to see what happens in a hospital lab:

pathologists to train their assistants—primarily young women—to perform some of the simpler laboratory procedures. Pathologists were now free to perform more advanced testing and procedures, such as autopsies and taking tissue samples.

The educational training of these women grew over time. In 1922, the American Society of Clinical Pathologists (ASCP) was formed to support the emerging clinical specialty of pathology. A tremendous leap in the evolution of the medical laboratory scientist career actually came in 1926, when the American College of Surgeons' accreditation standards called for all hospitals to have a clinical laboratory. These clinical labs had to be under the direction and supervision of a physician, preferably a pathologist.

In the early twentieth century, the need for laboratory assistants kept increasing, especially during World War I (1914–1918), when there was a critical shortage of laboratory assistants to staff the laboratories. This led to the creation of

Did You Know?

Every day, new advances in genetic testing, biomarkers, and PCR (polymerase chain reaction) technology are creating more job opportunities for clinical laboratory science professionals.

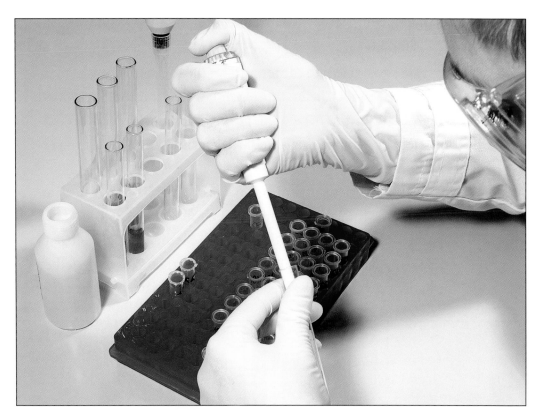

It toke many years for the medical community to recognize medical lab scientists as a legitimate medical profession.

a wide variety of training programs throughout the country to meet the growing call for these lab assistants. With the growth of these programs, a demand for standardization emerged.

In an effort to bring standardization to the education of laboratory personnel, ASCP created the Board of Registry (BOR) in 1928. This board was charged with certifying individual laboratory technicians, and soon after the Board of Schools (BOS) was established for the accreditation of educational programs. At this time individuals graduating from approved schools and passing the BOR's registry exam were then referred to as "medical technologists," or "MT (ASCP)." The ASCP at the end of the title was used to differentiate those trained by ASCP-accredited schools from those who were not. ASCP figured prominently in the development of the clinical laboratory science field by establishing standards for both education and certification.

In 1933, a new organization was formed—the American Society of Clinical Laboratory Technicians (ASCLT), later renamed the American Society of Medical Technologists (ASMT). Although ASMT and ASCP worked closely together for many years, they disagreed over several critical issues, espe-

Educational programs for medical lab scientists and technicians have improved greatly over the years to keep up with technological advancements in medicine.

"My Role Model"

A medical lab scientist was asked to describe the most rewarding aspect of her job. She commented:

"It is very rewarding when we are the first people to diagnose a serious illness. It could be working with a pathologist to find immature cells in a new leukemia case or getting chemistry results that might lead to a diagnosis of septicemia. It is rewarding to be able to know you help the patients without even seeing them."

cially the accreditation of schools and the certification of technologists, both of which ASCP still governed. In 1973, as a result of pressure from the U.S. Office of Education and the National Commission on Accrediting, ASCP agreed to disband the BOS and turn over its functions to an independently operated and governed board, the National Accrediting Agency for Clinical Laboratory Sciences (NAACLS). In 1977 a disagreement over the accreditation process prompted the ASMT to withdraw its representatives from the BOR and establish a separate certification agency, the National Certification Agency for Medical Laboratory Personnel (NCA). This opened the doors for clinical laboratory science to start achieving the status of an independent profession in the medical community.

The educational requirements and professional licensing for laboratory scientists has long been a topic debated within

Medical labs are constantly evolving and different technology is always coming into play.

the laboratory sciences field because of the gradual evolution of the career and its impact on the medical community. In 1930 when the ASCP issued the first certificates of registration, the requirements consisted of graduation from high school, completion of one year of classroom work, and six months of experience in a recognized laboratory. By 1952 most accredited schools required three years of college work, and ten years later, in 1962, the BOR formally increased the college prerequisite for what has become known as medical lab scientists to four years.

During the 1960s, new categories of laboratory workers

were created to help cope with the increased workload: the certified laboratory assistant (CLA), with one year of training, and the medical laboratory technician (MLT), with two years of training. In addition to the increase in educational requirements, specialist categories in chemistry, microbiology, hematology, and blood banking were also created. Later, master's and doctoral programs were put in place. This was to allow proper training of future clinical medical laboratory scientists and to fill faculty positions at accredited schools.

Today, it would be unheard of to discount the importance of medical laboratory scientists. With the constant evolution of medical research and technology, the need for medical lab scientists is growing daily.

 Text-Dependent Questions

1. How long does a certified laboratory assistant need to go to school for?
2. Where was the first "clinical lab" established?
3. Before medical laboratory scientists, who were performing diagnostic tests on patients?

 Research Project

Find out which medical laboratory was the first one established in your state, who founded it, and if it is still in business today.

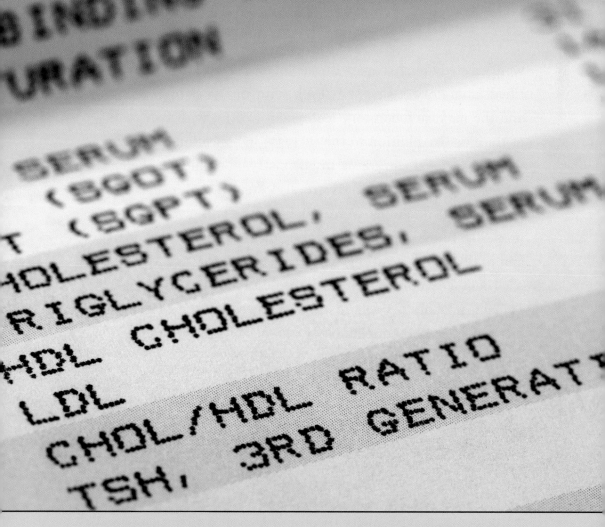

Blood screenings and analysis of other fluids play an important part in the process of medical diagnosis and treatment.

 Words to Understand in This Chapter

medical process—the process, from start to finish, by which a medical team works on specific patients to improve their health.

test methodology—the ways medical and diagnostic tests are created and performed.

5

Overview and Interview

Medical laboratory scientists are essential to the medical process. Diagnosing disease or just making sure a patient is healthy, medical laboratory scientists work hand and hand with other medical professionals on a daily basis. The laboratory analysis of blood and other bodily fluids is crucial to the diagnosis and treatment of disease, as well as to routine preventive medicine. In addition to performing a variety of laboratory examinations, medical laboratory scientists also help select and develop test methodology and instrumentation, establish and implement quality assurance programs, and promote technological advances. In addition, you can work in various types of labs. These labs may range

Medical laboratory scientists must be educated in all forms of science.

from industrial and pharmaceutical laboratories, to hospital, and physician's office laboratories. Medical lab scientists and technicians in all these labs work to improve the quality of life for people all around the world.

The history of medical laboratory science began in ancient Greece, where rudimentary examinations of human bodily fluids were initially conducted. The first recorded examination of bodily fluids dates back in the time of the ancient Greek physician Hippocrates, around 300 BCE. Not until 1896, however, was the first clinical laboratory established and opened. That laboratory was a 12-by-12-foot room at Johns Hopkins University Hospital that had equipment valued at around $50.

Before then, most "laboratories" consisted of a little corner in physicians' homes, offices, or hospital wards, where physicians themselves performed the bloodwork and different diagnostic testing procedures. Up until the early 1930s and 1940s, the value of laboratory testing was not fully appreciated, and many physicians did a lot of their testing themselves because they viewed clinical laboratories as an expensive luxury.

The critical need for clinical laboratories was first recognized during the devastating tuberculosis and cholera epidemics in the 1880s. As a result of these outbreaks, diagnostic tests were developed in the late 1890s for the detection of pathogens that caused the epidemics. This was a major step forward in the development of proper medical laboratories and ultimately the medical laboratory scientist profession itself.

Today, with rapidly evolving medical research and technology, medical professionals cannot imagine a health care system without the contributions of clinical or medical laboratory scientists. These scientists help establish and implement quality assurance programs, follow laboratory safety regimens, and troubleshoot technological and instrument malfunctions. Medical laboratory scientists

Educational Video

Scan here for a short video that offers reasons to choose MLS as a career:

also teach in university settings all over the country and around the world, preparing the next generation of medical laboratory technicians and scientists, and bolstering the clinical laboratory science field.

Medical laboratory scientists are required to complete an accredited medical laboratory bachelor's degree program. Then they obtain their licensure and can work in various laboratories.

There is a major difference between a medical laboratory scientist and a medical lab technician. While medical laboratory scientists—who complete four years of post-secondary education—can perform all tests and procedures physicians order, medical laboratory technicians—who generally obtain a two-year associate's degree or a certificate—cannot perform all these tests and usually work under the direct supervision of a medical laboratory scientist.

Q&A with a Professional in the Field

What follows is the transcript of an interview with Felicia Boehm, a medical laboratory scientist who works in a major hospital. Felicia discussed her career and how she thinks the profession will change over the next decade.

Felicia Boehm

Question: How long have you been a medical laboratory scientist?

Felicia: I was offered a job before graduation in May 2014. I began work under my MT licensure in June 2014.

What inspired you to go into this field?

Felicia: I had been interested in both the science and medical fields. Originally, I had looked into nursing and forensics. I had decided that nursing was not for me since I wasn't a "people person." After speaking to several students in my university's forensics program, I learned that the majority of aspiring forensics scientists needed to obtain a PhD. I decided to look into different majors and came across medical technology. I researched the major online and spoke to several students and professors in the program. I knew that it was the right fit for me.

What is your specialty and why did you choose it?

Felicia: I started as a generalist and did not have a specialty. However, hematology is my favorite. I love to be able to give a helpful diagnosis for the doctor. Sometimes, we are the first ones to know that a patient is severely anemic or has leukemia.

What has been the most challenging aspect of your job?

Felicia: Our job is always stressful. I work in a level-one trauma center that constantly has trauma patients coming in. We also have a children's, women's, and cancer unit. Many samples are urgent and are time-sensitive. Nurses and physicians are always calling the lab, looking for their results. It is hard to convey that there are 300 other chemistry tests running at the same time. Instruments also break down and you might have a coworker fixing them.

What would you say to a young adult considering MLS as a career?

Felicia: The schoolwork for an MLS is hard, but worth it. The field is always growing, and there are a lot of opportunities for a person with this degree. They can go into research, go into a specialty, work in management, etc.

What kind of personal traits do you think are important for an MLS?

Felicia: You must be patient, be able to work in a stressful environment, be able to multitask and prioritize tests. You must be able to communicate with a variety of health care professionals, including your coworkers, effectively.

Let's talk about the emotional side. Have you experienced traumatic events in your profession in which you have had to separate yourself from the sadness (i.e., of losing a patient or tending to a very sick child)? What kind of advice would you give new medical laboratory scientists on how to deal with this aspect of the job?

Felicia: Many times I have seen the loss of a patient whose specimens I have been dealing with for a long time. As an MLS, we regularly go on bone marrow aspirations. We see sick children and interact with their caregivers and their families. You see the patient's samples and know how their treatment is going, based on how their cells look. You also know how patients are doing by looking at their charts.

Felicia: You have to separate yourself from sad scenarios. You might have a patient who has a bad diagnosis or is living in a tough situation. As a medical professional, you have to remember that you are doing all that you can to help the patient and the work is rewarding.

MLS shifts are much different from those in the corporate world. Can you please explain the kinds of shifts an MLS is expected to work, and talk a little about the toll these shifts can take on your body, mind, and health as a whole?

Felicia: Shifts can be different, depending on where you work. An outpatient laboratory might have a typical 9-to-5 shift. Hospitals run 24/7 and can have shifts overnight, with some starting in the morning, around 6 a.m. Some hospitals allow 10- or 12-hour shifts. There isn't a "typical" shift. Every day is different. You might come into work one morning and find a computer down. Your coworkers might be staying there for longer than their scheduled 8-hour shift. Some shifts might be more stressful than others. Shifts can take a toll on your body, physically and mentally.

Explain being on call. How does that work for an MLS?

Felicia: I have never officially been on call; however, I have been called in on my days off work. I have also stayed overtime at work if a coworker has called in sick. Some part-time shifts include being on call.

Who do you look up to in your profession and why?

Felicia: I look up to the senior technologists I work with. They have been working in the field for longer than I have been alive. They have seen a lot and have been teaching students and coworkers for years. They have a lot to teach.

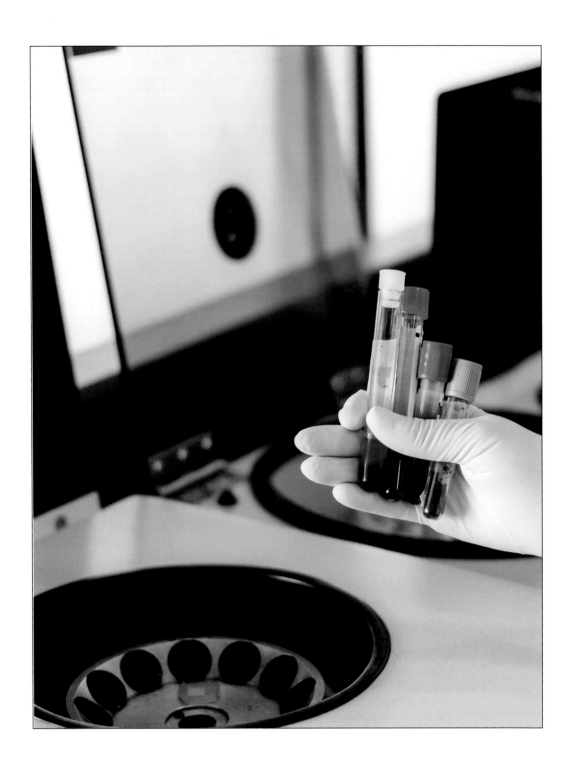

What kind of technology do you use each day?

Felicia: Each department uses a lot of technology. Our chemistry department uses an automated line to spin specimens and bring them to each instrument. After being sampled, it is brought to the next necessary instrument or a refrigerated stockyard. The chemistry department uses several technologies, like ISEs [ion selective electrodes], spectrophotometry, and immunoassays. Hematology uses coulters and coagulation uses technology bases on the detection of a clot or the absorbance of a color. Urinalysis uses technology to let us view pictures of the urine sediment enlarged on a screen. Microscopes are used throughout the laboratory.

Is this job what you expected when you first made the decision to get into this field?

Felicia: Yes, this is the job I expected.

What kind of income can a MLS expect to make starting out? Similarly, what does an established MLS typically make?

Felicia: The pay rate of an MLS is going to depend on many things. Location is a main factor. It will also depend on the shift that the person takes. Starting right out of college, an MLS can expect to make around $20–$22 an hour, or more, depending on past experience. You can get merit raises, shift differentials, extra for being a lead tech, etc. Some techs might make more working in other specialized fields, like cellular therapy, closer to $28 an hour.

In your mind, what makes for a successful career?

Felicia: You are successful in your career when you feel that you have made a difference. You can make a difference in the lives of your coworkers and your patients. You can help teach people from past experiences and knowledge. We all learn from our mistakes. You are successful if people look up to you.

 Text-Dependent Questions

1. What are some different types of labs where medical laboratory scientists can work, other than hospital labs?
2. What kind of diagnostic testing can a medical laboratory scientist do?
3. What makes the medical laboratory scientist who is interviewed feel as if she has had a successful career?

 Research Project

Locate the nearest clinical medical lab, and ask to interview a medical laboratory scientist firsthand. Then compare that interview to the interview transcribed here.

Series Glossary

accredited—a college or university program that has met all of the requirements put forth by the national organization for that job. The official stamp of approval for a degree.

Allied Health Professions—a group of professionals who use scientific principles to evaluate, diagnose and treat a variety of diseases. They also promote overall wellness and disease prevention in support of a variety of health care settings. (These may include physical therapists, dental hygienists, athletic trainers, audiologists, etc.)

American Medical Association (AMA)—the AMA is a professional group of physicians that publishes research about different areas of medicine. The AMA also advocates for its members to define medical concepts, professions, and recommendations.

anatomy—the study of the structure of living things; a person and/or animal's body.

associate's degree—a degree that is awarded to a student who has completed two years of study at a junior college, college, or university.

bachelor's degree—a degree that is awarded to a student by a college or university, usually after four years of study.

biology—the life processes especially of an organism or group.

chemistry—a science that deals with the composition, structure, and properties of substances and with the transformations that they undergo.

cardiology—the study of the heart and its action and diseases.

cardiopulmonary resuscitation (CPR)—a procedure designed to restore normal breathing after cardiac arrest that includes the clearance of air passages to the lungs, mouth-to-mouth method of artificial respiration, and heart massage by the exertion of pressure on the chest.

Centers for Disease Control—the Centers for Disease Control and Prevention (CDC) is a federal agency that conducts and supports health promotion, prevention and preparedness activities in the United States with the goal of improving overall public health.

diagnosis—to determine what is wrong with a patient. This process is especially important because it will determine the type of treatment the patient receives.

diagnostic testing—any tests performed to help determine a medical diagnosis.

EKG machine—an electrocardiogram (EKG or ECG) is a test that checks for problems with the electrical activity of your heart. An EKG shows the heart's electrical activity as line tracings on paper. The spikes and dips in the tracings are called waves. The heart is a muscular pump made up of four chambers.

first responder—the initial personnel who rush to the scene of an accident or an emergency.

Health Insurance Portability and Accountability Act (HIPAA)—a federal law enacted in 1996 that protects continuity of health coverage when a person changes or loses a job, that limits health-plan exclusions for preexisting medical conditions, that requires that patient medical information be kept private and secure, that standardizes electronic transactions involving health information, and that permits tax deduction of health insurance premiums by the self-employed.

internship—the position of a student or trainee who works in an organization, sometimes without pay, in order to gain work experience or satisfy requirements for a qualification.

kinesiology—the study of the principles of mechanics and anatomy in relation to human movement.

Master of Science degree—a Master of Science is a master's degree in the field of science awarded by universities in many countries, or a person holding such a degree.

obesity—a condition characterized by the excessive accumulation and storage of fat in the body.

pediatrics—the branch of medicine dealing with children.

physiology—a branch of biology that deals with the functions and activities of life or of living matter (as organs, tissues, or cells) and of the physical and chemical phenomena involved.

Surgeon General—the operational head of the US Public Health Department and the leading spokesperson for matters of public health.

Further Reading

Baker, F. J., R. E. Silverton, and Eveline D. Luckcock. *An Introduction to Medical Laboratory Technology*. London: Butterworth & Co (Publishers) Ltd, 2014.

Exton, John H. *Crucible of Science: The Story of the Cori Laboratory*. New York: Oxford University Press, 2013.

Ochei, J., and A. Kolhatkar. *Medical Laboratory Science: Theory and Practice*. New Delhi: Tata McGraw-Hill Education, 2000.

Internet Resources

www.ascls.org/what-is-a-medical-laboratory-science-professional
The website of the American Society for Clinical Laboratory Science provides information about the MLS profession.

www.bls.gov/ooh/healthcare/medical-and-clinical-laboratory-technologists-and-technicians.htm
This government website provides information on salaries and job outlook for medical and clinical laboratory scientists and technicians.

www.ncbi.nlm.nih.gov/pmc/articles/PMC164393/
An article on the history of medical lab science, as well as the outlook for the profession.

Index

Numbers in ***bold italic*** refer to captions.

About the Author

Samantha Simon has spent her career in healthcare: shadowing medical professionals, working in medical research, and as a patient liaison advocate within the industry. Her work authoring and writing about her experiences, and further studies into various aspects of the healthcare profession, has gained her unique insight into various aspects of the careers in the field of healthcare. Samantha received her Bachelor's Degree in Health Sciences Pre- Clinical Studies at the University of Central Florida. She has written and studied extensively in Neurobiology, Microbiology, Physiology, and Epidemiology, as well as worked on Medical Self-Assessment, Health Laws and Ethics, and Research Methods. She enjoys authoring and mentoring and lives in South Florida with her family and friends.